Quick Guide to Overcoming Sleep Problems: For Time-Deprived and Sleep-Deprived Parents

For Tired Parents Who Want More Personal Time to Themselves & Never Need to Wake Up in the Middle of the Night Again

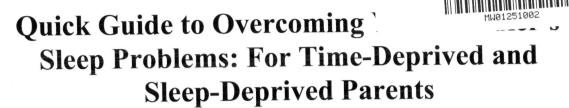

Quincy Kohler

TABLE OF CONTENT

Introduction

Welcome to *Quick Guide to Overcoming Your Toddler's Sleep Problems: For Time-Deprived and Sleep-Deprived Parents*. We're going to make sure that by the time you're done with this book, you'll have all the tools you need to get your little one to sleep with no fuss and on time.

Toddlers are challenging enough, but bedtime can often mean an extra struggle that leaves them, and often us too, exhausted. So why is bedtime such a struggle? As adults, we should certainly understand the drive behind not going to bed when we're tired. In fact, we often live our lives tired so understanding how a toddler can fight against sleep seems totally baffling. While it's normal toddler behavior to fight sleep a little, if your child is constantly causing trouble whenever you need them to rest you can often find yourself frustrated and disheartened. Fear not.

Quick Guide to Overcoming Your Toddler's Sleep Problems: For Time-Deprived and Sleep-Deprived Parents uses techniques described by some of the world's best pediatricians as guaranteed to make your child fall asleep fast.

You would be amazed how many parents struggle through ages 0-5 with little to no sleep just because they don't understand what is causing the problem. Congratulations on not being one of them!

This book will help you not only understand your child better but anticipate the problems and head them off before they happen. It will give you tools to deal with tired tantrums, unwanted cosleepers, that extra 15 minutes of "I need" before finally succumbing, and more.

If you want to win the battle against your toddler you need the tools we're going to give you. By the time you're done, you'll not only be glad you bought this book, but you'll be telling every other toddler parent you know just how you manage to sleep through the night, every night.

Chapter 1 – What Causes Sleep Problems?

Maybe you're already tried everything to get your child to sleep; maybe you've listened to all the advice, or you're determined that your child is "different". While we all believe our child is special, all toddlers have many behavioral similarities. Fighting against sleep is far more widespread than you would believe. There are several extremely common reasons why toddlers don't fall asleep when they should.

- not having a proper bedtime routine

- being unable to self-soothe

- being independent

- being codependent

- separation anxiety

- and over-stimulation

Just knowing what is causing your toddler's issues is a start on the road to fixing the problem. Think about the times you're having a battle, are they all the same or is it different each time? Many toddlers will have two or three issues from this basic list, seemingly without reason. If you've had the perfect baby but now have the terrible toddler when it comes to sleep, then there is scientific research as to what causes your baby to sleep great when your toddler won't.

Understanding your Toddler's Sleep

Just like adults, toddlers have phases of tiredness and sleep. While we might recognize them in ourselves picking them out in a toddler can be hard. Throughout the night whenever we sleep we actually cycle through different sleep phases, and it may be during a specific phase that your toddler experiences wakefulness. The four phases all humans experience when falling asleep are:

- drowsiness

- light sleep

- REM (rapid eye movement) sleep

- deep sleep

The most common time to wake up is during a transition such as that between light sleep and REM sleep. While you can't stop this happening what you can do is make sure that they remain in bed and fall peacefully back to sleep again. The brain is still active while we're sleeping and many of the processes that take place during sleep are vital to our well-being. Throughout our sleep we cycle between stage 2 and 4 but, as adults, we need about an hour and a half to do this while our toddler only needs 60 minutes.

Stage 1 sleep is that time between drowsiness and light sleep and is about 5-10% of the total time spent asleep; the problem is that it's very easy to be woken during light sleep. Stage 1 is normally the period when toddlers are woken, as anything untoward happening during this time is programmed into us to cause awakening. While we no longer have to be vigilant in our sleep for predators like our long lost ancestors our brains are still programmed to respond the same way. This is obviously a problem with children because they haven't learned that unless the house is burning down, it isn't time to wake up just because they've opened their eyes. The biggest issue with this for parents is often not the waking but the resettling afterward. Many children struggle with settling back down more than the initial sleep period. Don't worry; we'll tackle that too.

Stage 2 sleep is about 50% of the total amount of sleep and is still fairly light; it's easier to awaken during this period but once you reach a deep sleep if can be difficult to wake up. It's often that awakening during a deep sleep period means we have no memory of the event. Stage 3, which is the first stage of deep sleep, is REM where dreaming occurs. It is unlikely that your child will wake during this period of deep sleep.

Stage 4 is the deepest phase of sleep but only accounts for 25-35% of actual sleep. During deep sleep your blood pressure drops, the brain releases chemicals to still muscle and eye movement, and body temperature also drops. If you've ever started awake with a feeling of falling this was during deep sleep. It's hard to wake up during this phase, but because the brain is releasing different chemicals this can be a problem time. Deep sleep is usually where bedwetting, sleepwalking, and night terrors occur. The brain is, in theory, releasing chemicals to keep them asleep and in bed, but since the brain is still developing it may misunderstand the chemical signals. These cross wires mean that while the brain knows the bladder is full, and the child needs to wake too much of the sleep paralysis chemicals have been released to cause the child to wake up. Similarly, sleepwalking can mean that not enough of the sleep paralysis chemicals have been released, but the brain is not releasing any chemicals to wake them up.

Nighttime Wakefulness – YOU are the enemy

While brief wakefulness during sleep time is normal the biggest problem when trying to get them to sleep through the night is being unable to get back to sleep. If you've already got a good sleep routine going, you've already got the basic tools needed to combat this problem. When children awaken and see familiar objects, they are soothed just by their presence and often fall back to sleep easily. The problem arises when you are that familiar object and are not there, they panic and immediately cry out to bring you. Many of the associations they have with bedtime can be used to lull them right back into sleep mode again. For example, if they are used to falling asleep being rocked then they may become dependent on that to fall asleep. While you want the quickest solution simply rocking them is reinforcing the behavior rather than teaching them to soothe and return to sleep without you. You only have two choices here – cry or not to cry.

The biggest problem with the crying option is that it can disturb the whole household, meaning not only you but any other children are losing sleep. The trickiest phase is when this happens, and you'll need to use something called sleep training. What you're doing is for the long-run and will ultimately help them to fall back to sleep without you. If your child cries, it is instinctive to pick them up and soothe them. This can mean that they associate crying with being rewarded, and often this is the case. When they wake and panic that you're not there they cry which means you magically appear and soothe them back to sleep. They expect this to happen because you have created the routine, and when it doesn't they cry worse to force the action. This is instinctive and deliberate, so the only way to challenge this behavior is to create a new routine.

The key to this period is being supportive, and the whole family has to be involved and understanding that this is temporary. Older children make this more difficult than anything else but with the right reinforcement and retraining it won't last long. There is always going to be a division between the "cry" and "not to cry" camps. Personally, crying for a few nights if it means you'll ultimately get a full night's sleep faster seems a worthy pay off.

The Sleep Journal

Before taking any more steps, create a journal for your toddler's sleep. This is going to help you narrow down the problem and what is causing it. You'll need to assess your toddlers sleep and note down their activities before sleeping. If anything unusual or exceptional happens during the day (even if it's just a weekly visit from Grandma) note it down. If you have the patience, or your toddler sleeps well almost all nights, then do this for a week, noting specifically anything that might be affecting their sleep routine. In the end, if you still can't get your toddler to sleep using our methods this journal will give you the information necessary for a doctor to better understand what is going on. Start your journal with a few simple questions like these:

- Age/DOB

- Type of Delivery

- Health or developmental problems

- Medications

- Child's normal temperament

- Are they potty trained?

- Child's appetite/problems or concerns over eating habits

- Own/sibling shared room

- Own bed/Cosleeping

- Favorite Activities

- Other people/pets in the household

- What is the problem?

- When did it start?

- What do you think is causing it?

- Have there been any recent changes or stressors in your toddler's life?

- What have you already tried? Did they work?

Once you've created this simple assessment, you'll have a lot of information which you can match up with the techniques we're about to show you. Create a diary with each day marked off by the hour. Mark bedtime, what time they fall asleep, what time they awaken, if you gave them food or they needed the bathroom, and what time they awoke in the morning. Within a day or two you should notice a pattern. If you're not seeing a pattern, then you may have just found the simplest cure to your toddler's sleep issues.

Chapter 2 – Simple Problems and Solutions

Now that you've found out more about how your toddler's day and night breaks down you can start to analyze what you're seeing. While many of these issues can be tackled before they happen if you're seeing them in your journal then you need to tackle them NOW. The longer your child repeats their behavior, the harder it is to change. Dr. Hannah Chow of Loyola University ("https://www.loyolamedicine.org/doctor/hannah-chow") wrote a detailed paper on how sleep problems can affect behavior throughout the day and toddler health. Sleep matters. Check your journal for these common problems and solutions and see if you can identify any of them in your toddler.

The Early Riser

While your child might have no problem being awake at 6 am, you may not want to be. Early awakening is a very common problem, and it has a lot to do with the fact that children have shorter sleep cycles than adults. They are refreshed in much less time than we are because their inner clock runs a bit faster. While their bedroom might be the perfect place to fall asleep, it can also be a challenging place to stay asleep. The problem of awakening in the night can also be part of the problem why they're awakening in the morning. Even if your child wakes up bright and early you want them to try and fall back to sleep until a more reasonable time.

The Solution: Have a look at your child's room when they awaken. Is there something that has changed around this time that might cause them to awaken? One of the easiest things to miss is that children are used to sleeping when it's dark, and while we can look at a clock they associate daylight with "awake time". If they need the nightlight at night make sure that you opt for a timed one or a changing color alarm clock that only changes color when it's time to awaken. Your child needs to associate sleep time and wake time differently. If the room is too light when they wake up, then consider opting for heavier drapes to block out more light which will keep the room darker. If there is street noise, consider sending them to sleep with a noise machine so that they become accustomed to sleeping even when there is some background noise. An earlier bedtime may also have an effect by putting them into a different, deeper, phase of sleep during the time when they usually awaken.

No-Nap Nancy

Are you fighting to keep nap time? Nap time can be one of the most frustrating time because it's easy to skip and hard to schedule, especially if you're balancing sibling needs as well. While ideally your toddler needs a nap you'll often count it as optional when it should be a necessity. If your toddler is fighting nap time (when it does happen) it can mean that they no longer have the routine where it's required. It's harder to get your child to nap if they're not used to it. Not only this but being over-tired can make them fight sleep even more which can create a cascade with problems at bedtime as well. *The Solution:* If your toddler is in dire need of a nap (refer to your journal and see if they're exhibiting signs of tiredness during the day at particular times) then make that part of their daily schedule. Just as older siblings have school schedules your toddler needs the same daily routine, especially if you want to cultivate better sleeping habits. Start bedtime a little earlier to make up for any sleep deficit they have already, then during the day make sure they are properly tired out before nap time. About an hour before you want them to take a nap give them some downtime without excessive stimulation to help them calm and then put them down at a designated time. Once you've established the nap routine during the day, you can move it around and make it a little more flexible but try to keep morning and afternoon naps as specific and separate times.

The Fighter

We are all guilty of fighting tiredness to stay awake. Sometimes your toddler isn't just fighting tiredness but is genuinely having trouble falling asleep because they're so overstimulated they physically can't. While activities and play can be the perfect way to tire them out it can also wind them up to the point where they struggle to relax and soothe enough to reach drowsiness. They're so focused on all the things going on that they don't notice they are drowsy. While you might notice it, they don't, and so you have a fight on your hands as they can't understand why they are being forced (against their will) to do something they see as unnecessary. This can also be a side effect of not having a proper sleep routine set up.

The Solution: Having a dedicated sleep routine at bedtime can help reinforce the behavior that it's time to sleep, just as with nap time. You'll want to make sure they are aware of their drowsiness, so they have less trouble reaching light sleep. (This works well for older children too) Turn off electronics for at least 60 minutes before bedtime and let them play quietly or read to them. Story time before bed is an ideal way to relax and calm down so that they can physically feel drowsy and even reach light sleep. While it can be difficult to allot the time for this it is essential if your child is fighting bedtime to give them this down time.

The Needy One

We have all encountered that child that just won't let go at bedtime. No matter how quietly you leave the room, or how much grandma wants to be the one to put them to bed they just won't let anyone else put them to sleep. You have created a routine where your child depends on your presence to sleep; you have become their teddy-bear. Some children can be especially difficult to soothe if they have become too dependent on you. What you want to do is to cultivate their ability to soothe themselves and transfer their dependence onto an item that can sleep with them through the night. This will not only free you up to be elsewhere it can help them fall back to sleep at night by seeing that soothing item without waking you.

The Solution: If your child is determined to be held to fall asleep start shortening the time you're holding them, on day one put them down in their bed or crib and remain touching them; between days 1-3 sit next to the crib or lay close to them but not touching. Gradually increase your distance for them as they fall to sleep. For example, sit a chair close by the bed, then move it to the middle of the room, then to the doorway, and then outside of the room so they can hear you but not see you. What this does is allow them to be aware of your presence without your being physically connected to them.

If your child already has a favorite teddy or blanket then simply having it at bedtime can be soothing, but if they haven't found that "one" object yet you need to provide it. For example, my mother made a small quilt out of my dad's old shirts. Not only did it smell like my dad but the feel of it was similar to that of being held because of the shirt texture. This blanket was the substitute for my father having to hold me to make me sleep because I transferred my need to have him there to the blanket. While you might not be as nifty with a sewing machine having an object there that the child associates with you and with bedtime can help transfer their need for you onto the object. Jennifer Mettter, a Certified Sleep Consultant swears by these transferable items as the best method to get a toddler to sleep through the night if they struggle with self-soothing.

Can I have.....

Bedtime might be at 8 pm, but your toddler isn't actually in bed and attempting sleep until 8.30. Asking for "one more thing" is a perfect delay tactic to stay up longer. We want our child to sleep so we pander to these demands to quickly get them there. The problem is that we're making the problem worse. We *know* when bedtime is, yet when it rolls around, and we know we will have this extra time of demands we still cater to them. This extra awake time can often cause your child to become overtired which adds its own problems which can cascade over into the next day. Refer to your sleep journal, has your child got the same routine of demands? A glass of water, the bathroom, a snack, a song?

The Solution: "Good night" needs to mean just that. Your journal should show you all the needs and demands that your toddler comes up with to put off sleep, so what you're going to do is anticipate them. If they always ask for a glass of water, make sure it's already waiting and included in the bedtime routine. If they always ask you to sing a song, start bedtime 5 minutes earlier to accommodate it. If they want a hug, etc. Create an earlier bedtime so that they are in bed and ready to sleep at the designated time you want. If they're still not getting the message, then you'll need to create a "good night" signal since the words have lost their meaning. Start with the earlier bedtime to accommodate the needs/wants and then set a timer for 15 minutes. Explain that they have 15 minutes before they must be tucked in and trying to sleep. You can also implement consequences if they don't stick to it. For example, if they are determined to have a song or one more hug you can tell them there won't be time for it if they aren't in bed before the timer goes off.

The Co-Sleeper

While the "big bed" can be daunting having an unwanted co-sleeper can be a tough one to crack. There are several reasons behind why your child wants to get into bed with you, not only that but the fact that you may not wake up until morning means that they have spent the entire night with you without your realizing. In this instance, you'll need to refer to your journal to determine what is causing them to leave their bed. Is it a need for your presence? Is their bed comfortable? Is it because they are seeing sleeping in your bed as a reward for waking up?

The Solution: First, check that your child is genuinely comfortable in bed. We've all been plagued by an uncomfortable mattress, and this is an easy solution to miss when you're focused on their emotional and physical well-being. If they see it as a reward, simply return them to bed quietly and without fuss as soon as you notice them in your bed. Be consistent with this, even if they fuss they must return to their own bed. Your child won't continue to try if they realize that they're not going to get their way. If they're waking up and coming to your bed because they need your presence, then look at the solution for the needy child and see about getting a transference object.

Chapter 3 – Before Getting Ready for Bed

While it's easy to say that sleep problems have simple solutions many sleep plans fail because parents ignore signs that are terribly obvious. When you did your assessment, you noted down issues and problems that your child has. We're now going to look at them and see if any of them is preventing the child from being able to have a good night's sleep so that your sleep training method can be effective.

Health

Is your child healthy enough for a good night's sleep? The biggest issue you're going to run across is teething. In the acute teething phase of their lives, they are going to be in constant discomfort which is going to lead to fussy behavior and general crankiness. Unfortunately, this can't be helped, and you're going to have to accept that training your child to sleep through the night at this time isn't going to be successful. Other issues could include reflux, medication side effects, allergies, or a cold. If your child has any health issues, consult their pediatrician about getting them better sleep.

Weight

A subheading of health, if your child is healthy enough to go without midnight feedings, you may be able to skip them. Most pediatricians advise waiting until at least five months so your toddler should be well past this time. As long as they weigh over 14lb, they are capable of sleeping through the night without a feeding without adverse effects.

If you're looking to wean them off, you'll want to include that in their schedule. Ideally, you should change from one large feeding to smaller ones. This can be done over the course of 5 nights with relative ease. This is an ideal sample schedule:

Night 1	Night 2	Night 3	Night 4	Night 5
7pm Bedtime	7pm Bedtime	7pm Bedtime	7pm Bedtime	7pm Bedtime
9.30pm Feed 4oz	9.30pm Feed 3oz	9.30pm Feed 2oz	9.30pm Feed 1oz	
2.30am Feed 3oz	2.30am Feed 2oz	2.30am Feed 1oz		
6am Awake	6am Awake	6am Awake	6am Awake	6am Awake

As you reduce the amount they feed in the night, you can offer them more during the day so that they continue to take in the same amount but at a more convenient time. For older children a small snack before bedtime is acceptable as long as it does not have sugars or caffeine which will keep them awake.

Transition

Children learn and grow everyday; it's often difficult to remember how exciting each day life can be as a child. Learning new milestones is like winning the lottery for your toddler, only it happens every day. Every time they learn something new they are going to be incredibly excited. They're going to want to practice that new skill and often they won't feel like sleeping because this new thing is more exciting. Not only that but they can often feel great anxiety at this time as they notice the distance between you and them. While you may have had to hold them constantly as a baby, their independence is pulling them away, and so they feel a certain amount of separation anxiety. Children in a transitioning phase will often experience sleep problems. The right calming method before bed will help eliminate both the excess energy and the anxiety of separation.

Another example of a transition can be something new in their routine. For example, if mom is transitioning back to work. This is something that can cause a lot of anxiety; it can also affect a mother's milk if she is breastfeeding which in turn is passed on to the child. Sleep training cannot be effective at this time because there is simply too much for the child to absorb, wait until you are more settled and able to create a routine.

Scheduling

A good sleep schedule is one you can stick to. With siblings and busy lives flexible scheduling is something we have to adapt to. The problem is that toddlers don't work well on a flexible schedule. Prioritize their schedule while they are learning to sleep. The week you plan on implementing training is a little sacrifice for sleeping through the night from thereon. When you have created your sleep plan for your child, stick to it exactly as this will reinforce the behavior. Consider starting your schedule on a weekend to give you a little extra flexibility and practice in those first two days.

Include Everyone

Siblings and caregivers can often be the silent sabotage to even the most well-laid plans. Ensure that any caregivers that will be responsible for nap time or bed time are aware, on board, and able to stick with the schedule you provide. If your caregiver is using alternative methods, this might just be the problem since they are interrupting the routine to implement their own. Make sure they have written and detailed instructions to follow and make frequent contact with them over the process. The same goes with your other children; they may find the baby exciting and wish to play while it is toddler sleep time. There need to be clearly defined rules allowing your toddler to stay on the schedule that will also apply to your other children. There have been plenty of instances where parents do everything, only to find out that an older sibling or pet is sneaking in and waking the child at night. Don't forget the pets too!

If you've covered all of these, your sleep assessment has no other issues, and your pediatrician has no medical reasons why your toddler shouldn't sleep through the night then you are ready to implement your sleep training plan.

Chapter 4 – Sleep Routine Planning

There's a good chance you've noticed that almost all toddler sleep problems have something to do with their routine. Whether it's their routine of awakening early, being rewarded for being out of bed, or fighting naps. Your child needs routine. What you want to do is to look at your journal and determine what you need to create a successful sleep plan for them. This chapter is dedicated to the information you need to do just that.

Bedtime Timing

While you might be inclined to let your child dictate their schedule, especially if they have such an obvious one (look at your sleep journal), you need to anticipate the tired times rather than cater to them. Allowing your child to reach the stage of being tired while still being active, and stimulated means they may be tired but not able to sleep. If they continue to be active the brain releases cortisol. This hormone acts like adrenaline and caffeine and will keep them awake. Time your sleep plan based on when they start to get tired and not when they are already tired. If you've been thorough with your journal, you'll notice certain symptoms in a tired child that should signal sleep time is imminent. These include:

- resistance to eye contact

- lack of interest or interaction

- a glazed look

- zoned out behavior

Note when these start to occur and plan bedtime for 15-30 minutes beforehand so that they are already in bed or getting to bed at the optimum time. On your schedule create a time that is "bedtime" and then count 11 hours forward to "wake up". You can also mark this on a non-digital clock in their room in colors (green for awake, red for sleep time), make sure the hands are clear enough for the child to understand or consider the color changing alarm clock previously mentioned.

How Long?

A toddler needs to sleep about 11 hours, and while it may not be convenient for you that they stay up/wake up at certain times, you need to balance that 11 hours with your 8. While there's about a 30-minute window either way for most children, you need to be able to schedule that time on your sleep plan. Once you've tackled nighttime issues so that they're sleeping through the night, this is going to be the next step so try and fit their naps and bedtime into that schedule already, and you won't need to cause any adjustment or upheaval once that time comes. Make sure you don't let the child sleep more than 12 hours as this will often mean they don't have enough time to get tired again for a nap and may cause you to skip it.

Make a Sleep Book

Kids love story time and picture books, especially visual children. Even if you're no artist stick figures can be enough to explain the process they are about to go through. Ask them to help color in the pictures or draw themselves doing the actions needed in the plan. This will help to teach them the process in a way that they can see themselves doing the actions and going to sleep. Make sure you use their name often in the book, so they know that the book relates to them. You can read this as a story book to them during their nightly routine to help familiarize them with the process and make changes less sudden. Here is an example:

"Mommy & Daddy are going to help Tommy learn to sleep! Tommy needs sleep because without enough rest he can't play during the day. Oh no! (picture of your child feeling sad because they can't play). After dinner, we have a bath and wrap up warm in pajamas. (picture of your child in pajamas). Then Mommy puts you in bed (picture), Daddy reads you a story (picture)...................

Have the Child Pick their Transition Item

By including the child in the process, you're ensuring they don't hate the item and refuse to use it. I hated bears as a child, didn't want them near me which is why the blanket my mother made was so ideal. Potential transition items to replace you need to be acceptable for bed-time and not something stimulating they can play with. Consider a bear to "replace" Mommy (obviously use a better term such as "reminds you of") that they can sleep with or a special blanket. It's important to offer your child choices, so they feel they have some element of control in the process.

Potential Problems with this include the fact that blankets and stuffed toys may cause a risk of suffocation or choking. You want a blanket that is breathable (you can cover your face with it and still breathe through it) and is no more than 12" square so they cannot become trapped or tangled in it. There's no guarantee that any item in their sleep area is safe so use these with caution. If your child needs a pacifier to sleep and awakens when they can't find it you may need to add a few spares into their sleep area. Place them in a bowl beside the bed or close by in the crib if they are capable of reinserting them themselves. If your child is dependent on you to reinsert it, then it can become a sleep association that if they cry, you'll come to do that.

Limit-Testing Tactics

Now that you've identified potential problems that may be causing your problems, you also need to identify your child's delay tactics. While you know they throw tantrums; you may not have noticed that they also ask for water or use you as a sleep aid. Look at your sleep journal and make sure you are aware of all of the problems that your child exhibits so that you don't tackle one without addressing the other. On your sleep planner write their typical tactics to avoid sleep. You can also create a chart in their bedroom then explain that if he or she goes to bed without a tantrum, they will get a sticker. Or if they go to bed on time they get their favorite breakfast etc. Identifying all of their tactics is a great way to "know your enemy" better than they know themselves as most children prefer positive reinforcement methods and will realize quickly that they aren't getting their way.

Writing the Plan/Before "Go" time

By now you should have plenty of information on your child's sleeping habits to know what to include in your plan for a successful schedule. A good plan takes all these important elements into account plus anything specific to your child:

- Daytime Naps/Enough playtime to be tired

- Winding down time (60mins) before bedtime

- Anticipating needs/wants before reaching bedtime (list them if necessary)

- Reinforcement with the sleep book & inclusion of child in pre-planning

- Making sure all caregivers are on board/have copies and that they are nearby for reference at night.

- Review the plan before "go night"

- Implement any necessary changes like buying darkening curtains or a sleep machine.

- Include Check-in times for your peace of mind and to break up bad behavior

At this point, you should be ready and well prepared for your first night of sleep training.

Chapter 5 – Go Time

On the night you plan on starting sleep training, create an easily accessible station. This station should be in your bedroom or the living room and definitely outside of the child's bedroom. You'll want your sleep journal, a copy of your plan, a digital clock, a pen/pencil, tissues, the baby monitor (if it's not next to your bed), and any other items you think you will need on hand at night to make things run smoothly.

Step 1: Implement the Routine

You made a plan; now you must stick to it. Do not let your child get into the same habits, make sure you are fully focused on them so you can notice the drowsiness coming on and implement bedtime ASAP. If they are becoming drowsy while feeding or during bath time then wrap it up and make them move more, don't allow them to sleep until the designated time. If you have left 11 hours in your plan for their sleep, they may still be overtired the first day or two but stick with your plan! Make sure you let the child know that it is "go" time, and give supporting words "it may be hard, but I know you can do it" etc. Don't forget to use the sleep book.

Step 2: Bedtime

The clock is ticking, make sure you refer to all those need and tactics that need to be dealt with beforehand. Your child needs to be awake but tired at this time so they are aware of the process and can take it in. Remind them with supportive words that they can do this and that you love them. Be firm against those limit-testing tactics and use the rewards you set out if necessary. You need to be firm or your toddler's biological clock won't kick in with repetition.

Step 3: Leave!

This is the hardest step. You're panicking, you're heartbroken, but you have to do it! If they're the needy child, you can make this a gradual step over several nights as previously suggested.

Step 4: Crying

Why is this a step? Because it's going to happen. There will always be bumps in the road at first. Learning the process is frustrating and as much as you want to soothe them and calm them down quickly you need to go against your instincts. A little crying will not emotionally damage your child and long-term sleep deprivation has far worse side-effects. Consistency is key to getting your child to stop crying. Be firm and use the same method each time they exhibit their behavior. While you might think they hate you now, they will still love you in the morning, promise. You'll usually find that this pattern changes quickly, within five nights or so according to Jennifer Waldburger of the Sleepeasy Solution ("http://www.sleepyplanet.com/").

Listen, acknowledge, and then implement your plan for a swift and silent return to sleep. If your plan is to let them cry it out for a few days, then you'll just have to let them cry it out until they figure it isn't getting them anywhere. Often you'll find they cry themselves out and go back to sleep but the first night can be hellish. Remember, think long-term.

During a crying episode if you absolutely must check in then keep it brief and reassuring. Don't hold or touch your child as this will reward the behavior. Try and stick it out until a designated check-in time on your schedule and stay for no more than 30 seconds. Be calm, but firm.

Step 5: Make notes

Using your journal, note down bedtime and any difficulty that your child had with your sleep routine. Were there tears? Did they try a new tactic? Were you successful? If you have to, you can do a quick 30-second check to make sure they're asleep but don't wake them. Try not to be glued to your monitor or outside their door waiting to see if the process works, distract yourself by enjoying the time as well as you can while they learn the process. Don't forget to record the amount of time they sleep and how long it took them to do so each night. Take your sleep station equipment with you if you're heading to bed or another room so that you can keep track of any occurrences.

The Next Step:

Within a few days, you should be able to note differences in your child's sleeping habits. Look for clues that they are adapting and learning such as not complaining or less crying. Try to check-in less as the days go on as this will help them progress. If you're caught checking in the child may see it as an excuse to fuss and get attention like they used to. If they're using new tactics like coming to your bed make sure you use the firm, calm, and swift concept to return them back to their bed each time. Eliminate as much talking as possible and be firm when the battle starts; they will not want to go back to bed easily. Stay consistent and any new behavior will soon stop. Do not get pulled in by any new tactics they use to stay awake longer and avoid caving into new demands.

Hopefully, you'll start seeing results within a few days and a full night's sleep in a week!

Chapter 6 – A Quick Word on Special Situations

Not all sleep problems are as simple as they seem. There are myriad different reasons why your child might be waking up or still awake. Special situations like vacations or visits are an ideal thing to derail your child's sleep, and many medical problems are hard to accurately diagnose without a sleep study. These are some of the special situations that pop up most frequently, but the last thing you want to do is run for medication according to the popular pediatrician Dr. Harvey Karp. When things aren't going right is when your child needs you the most.

Coughs, Allergies & Asthma

All kids get colds and about 40% experience allergies of some sort. These both trigger a cough that can only pop up during the night because of mucus in the throat. If a cold seems to drag on it may be more likely to be asthma or allergies. Several common causes include dust, mildew, cigarette smoke, paint fumes, and pollen.

Open the windows and ventilate the room while the child is awake. Make sure your vents have fresh filters and use hypoallergenic products. Do not allow smoking near your child and consider an antihistamine under your pediatrician's orders if necessary. Elimination diets and allergy shots may also help.

Asthma is its own problem as it affects breathing tubes deep within the chest. Breathing is labored and wheezy. Your child will sound and feel like a fish out of water. Asthma is no joke; it can quickly turn deadly and if you have any suspicion your child is suffering from asthma you need to see a doctor immediately. This is one of the times that medication can be lifesaving.

Another unusual, but possible, option is that your child may have inhaled something during daytime play that is obstructing their airway. Ask your doctor to check and be sure if your child has a very sudden cough.

Snoring and Chocking

Snoring can be cute, but if your toddler snores very regularly and has dark circles when waking and drools, you might find that your toddler has sleep apnea. Large tonsils at throat and obstructing adenoids or turbinate in nose aren't life-threatening and having them removed can be a clear and easy remedy to sleep issues. Post-surgery recovery rate for toddlers are amazingly fast within a week or two in most cases. Sleep-disordered breathing means the patient is having trouble getting enough air; this causes the child to cough and choke response to try and get as much air as possible. It can start as early as the toddler years and is something to watch for if your child's sleep isn't improving. Between 7-12% of children suffer from this. In fact, sleep apnea's problem is much more common in toddlers than we think. When you visit an ENT (Ear, Nose, Throat) specialist, referred by your physician due to repeated throat and nose problems faced by your toddlers, first question that the specialist will usually ask is "Does your child snore when they sleep?" The answer is almost yes in most cases where children has sleep problems.

Obesity

With the rising rate of child obesity, it's no wonder they're experiencing the same sleep problems as adults with the same issues. Fat builds up all over the body, and this includes behind the membranes in the nose and throat, narrowing the airways. Reducing junk food and a healthier diet as well as exercise can make a huge difference at such an early age. Reduce that regular amount of sweet food and drinks can reduce the over-stimulation and hyperactivity of your toddler before sleep.

Night Seizures

Night seizures can be as small as a body jerk or as severe as screaming and urination. Some bedwetting issues may be related to night seizures and some night terrors may be mistaken for more. If you're concerned your child is having seizures in their sleep, look for signs of drooling, twitching, tongue biting, and incontinence. With any concern, see a doctor immediately.

Autism and Development Issues

While many developmentally challenged children experience sleep issues they are often the quickest to find their own solution. Humming, spinning, and repetitive motions such as rocking are all great tools for calming an emotionally sensitive child. Research shows that children like this often sleep less than normal naturally, but using a heavy or weighted blanket has been shown to be one of the best tools for this.

Attention-deficit/hyperactivity disorder (ADHD) requires its own sub-paragraph because these hyperactive issues can affect a child's ability to sleep. Poor sleep has been linked to triggering hyperactivity, according to Dr. Karp, so consider treating the sleep issue if it does not go away.

Nightmares

Sleepwalking and nightmares come with their own brand of drama and are entirely linked to the chemicals of REM sleep. While most bad dreams and nightmares are chemical induced, they can still be scary. Try and determine if your toddler is angry, frustrated, or has seen something upsetting that may be causing this. Role-playing is a great way to help bring out any worries your toddler has and get to the bottom of what's causing this.

Conclusion

Getting your toddler to sleep can be a fight, and it's a fight you've lost in the past. Hopefully, you've learned some new tools and insight into what is causing the problem, no matter what it is. Remember, consistency and scheduling are the keys to successful planning, so you need to have your journal and plan to hand at all times once you pass "go".

- If your child is fighting nap time, consider an earlier bedtime and better schedule.

- If your child is an unwanted co-sleeper, send them quietly back to bed.

- If your child is putting off bedtime, be firmer about the rules.

- If your child is needy, stop rewarding their behavior with your presence.

You CAN do this. Remember the sleep training plan is meant for long-term success and even if your first week is hellish, you should swiftly see results with these methods.

Good luck getting better sleep, and remember to think long-term when you fight that instinct to comfort your little one.

Other Books You May Be Interested

Check out other book by Quincy Kohler.

Other book you may be interested in.

Made in the USA
Lexington, KY
22 March 2018